The ABCs of Entrepreneurs

Bryan Menell and Thom Singer

The ABCs of Entrepreneurs

New Year Publishing, LLC
144 Diablo Ranch Court
Danville, CA 94506 USA
orders@newyearpublishing.com
http://www.newyearpublishing.com

ISBN: 978-1935547174

To Angi, my children, and all of my family who put up with my crazy entrepreneur lifestyle. *–Bryan*

To Sara, Jackie and Kate. As always, thank you for all you do to support my crazy career as a speaker and author. *–Thom*

To all the entrepreneurs who have been part of our professional careers. Thanks for all the advice and examples to keep pushing for success.

Acknowledgements

Special thanks to:

Leslie Morris, our editor, for her keen insights and support throughout the project.

Mary Lance, our friend, who did the first reading of the book and for letting us know we were on the right track.

Bob Phelan, Thom's father-in-law, for his eagle eye in proofing the final manuscript.

Contents

Introduction

Welcome to the *ABCs of Entrepreneurs*. While entrepreneurship is not as easy as A-B-C, we hope that this book inspires and excites you about the realities and possibilities of working hard to grow your own business. While no two businesses, or the people who run them, are exactly the same, there are many commonalities that drive success.

Entrepreneurs launch and operate businesses, take risks, and create not only products and services, but jobs. All companies begin with an idea. Depending on the goals of the founders, employees and investors, some businesses grow into multi-national organizations while others remain small local ventures. There is no right answer on what the end goal of a business is, but an entrepreneur has the drive and the vision to strike out on their own. The spirit of entrepreneurship lives on in boom times and recessions, in big companies and small.

If you have a desire to start your own company you have to be clear about what it means to work for yourself, be the boss, manage employees, find investment capital, and many other things. This book will guide you in an understanding of the twists and turns that come with being an entrepreneur. It takes a lot of courage and hard work, but we believe the success is in the journey.

A is for Advisors

Surrounding yourself with good people is one of the most critical things you can do when you finally venture out and start your own company. Being an entrepreneur can feel mighty lonely in the beginning, especially coming from a team environment. Advisors can help fill that void.

A first step is to set up a formal board of advisors. A typical rookie maneuver is to ask friends or others you have an existing relationship with to be your advisors. Instead, work a little harder and line up the best advisors you possibly can. Do your research. Make a list of who would be best suited to advise you. Aim high. You may not get them, but it will jump-start your thought process about the types of people who might be attainable. If Bill Gates isn't returning your calls, think about who else out there really knows consumer marketing.

It's important to make this relationship formal. You will not get the full benefit of the advisory relationship from an accountant, lawyer or other person from whom you seek input without being specific about the expectation of their involvement.

Industry experts, potential investors and corporate executives are good choices. Seek people with solid business relationships, extensive industry knowledge and success. Consider someone with a proven track record who may be retired or active on the speaking circuit. If you're building a large computer services company, former IBM CEO Lou Gerstner would be both an ideal advisor and a potential investor. This is an extreme example, of course, but if you research your industry you can find people who have successfully sold their companies and would make a great advisor.

Corporate executives also make great advisors. You don't necessarily need FedEx's CEO but what about a lesser-known senior executive at FedEx with similarly deep industry insight? A little homework could really pay off.

"Having industry veterans on your advisory board" is a box you want to check on your "to-do" list in the early days. If you can recruit one or two solid, well-known advisors to your company, you might find recruiting the rest easier. Just as you are seeking their advice, these potential advisors are smart business people with limited time. They want to network with other smart people, so solid references and thoughtful name-dropping will help build a well-rounded and balanced team.

Setting expectations from the onset regarding compensation and time commitments will lead to stronger relationships. Typically you're going to pay your advisors with stock options in your new company. However, if they incur costs such as international calls or travel expenses, it's expected that you reimburse them. Establish quarterly conference calls with your whole advisory board and ad hoc calls with individual advisors when necessary.

A realistic term limit for an advisor is two years. Your company will be in a far different place two years from now so you should plan up front for different types of advisors as your needs change. If you plan and manage your advisors appropriately, they will provide years of value to you and someday you will be able to return the favor.

B is for Brainstorming

Ideas are paramount to success for an entrepreneur. Unfortunately, not all ideas are the right ideas for starting a business.

Some businesses are spawned from a single idea. However, most people who achieve sustainable success will need to consistently identify new concepts, products and services. To avoid becoming a One Hit Wonder, entrepreneurs must always be on the lookout for the New Thing either to grow their existing business or to launch their next venture.

Brainstorming, a process for developing creative solutions, can take many different forms. The concept was popularized in the 1950s and 1960s by Alex Osborn in his book *Applied Imagination.* Osborn proposed that teams could double their creative output through brainstorming techniques.

When a team of people works together, the end result is often stronger than any one person could achieve alone. Effective entrepreneurs do not operate in a vacuum. They are surrounded by people who allow them to expand beyond their own individual limitations. Collectively, they weave the best thoughts together to create powerful solutions.

Brainstorming involves a group of people focused on a problem and then coming up with as many solutions as possible. The purpose is to push the creative thought process with each person having the ability to expand on the ideas of others and combine concepts to create new ones.

The process can be both formal and informal, and it is important in the formation stage of a business as well as when tackling issues that can stall a company's ongoing growth. To continually have success, an entrepreneur must always look forward. Getting the whole team involved to create a culture where everyone is looking to add to the greater good of the company is paramount to success.

Once ideas are uncovered, there must be a system for deciding which should be acted upon. There is neither the time nor the resources available to act on every idea. Not all ideas will help move the company toward its goals. Focus and prioritize which ideas best support the company's mission. An entrepreneur's experience, instincts and trusted advisors all play a role in deciding which ideas to implement and how to do so.

Entrepreneurs must be willing to take risks while balancing the need to stay the course. Discovering the ideas, while important, is only part of the journey for anyone looking to grow a business. Without ideas, however, there is no foundation on which to build.

C is for Co-Founders

Finding other people to help start your company is one of the most challenging and rewarding things entrepreneurs must do. Done right, a solid group of co-founders can go on to dominate an industry, or even invent a new one. Done wrong, it's a business killer.

History is full of famous co-founders like Steve Jobs and Steve Wozniak, and Bill Hewlett and Dave Packard. Even solo company founder Michael Dell recruited four co-workers at a computer retailer to join Dell Computer.

Just like the brainstorming teams and advisors, there is strength in numbers and quality. While clearly you are smart, you're not so smart as to have cornered the market on all the good ideas in the world. Without feedback, collaboration and the energy that other people bring to your early stage company, success is more difficult. So, how many founders does it make sense to have and what types of people create the best founder formula?

When it comes to founders, odd numbers are good. Founding teams generally contain three or five people, and most often three. If two people start a company, what happens when they disagree? They can't flip a coin to see who gets to win each time. An odd number of founders ensures that there is always someone to break ties. Ideally, you all agree on the important things, but the reality is that it may not happen that way.

There are also three types of people who make good co-founders: makers, sellers and organizers. Each has its strengths, but needs the others to succeed.

> *Makers* build the product, bring their vision to reality and look for people to take on the tasks that they either don't want to do or know they're not good at doing.

> *Sellers* have deep industry knowledge, a clear understanding of the game-changing

offering, and contacts that are early potential customers.

Organizers are detail-oriented people looking for other co-founders. A team made up of these three personalities is a solid founding group. Personalities matter. Are they likeable? Can they disagree without being disagreeable? Are they genuinely nice people, and a pleasure to be around? Most importantly, are you able to have honest conversations together about the business and its challenges? Good co-founders are "get things done" people. They are motivated, make things happen with a sense of urgency and, no matter what the obstacles, produce and create at levels other people can't. Being demanding as an entrepreneur is usually required, however it's important to maintain what author Tim Sanders calls "The L Factor, Likeability." in his The L-Factor book.

Once you identify a potential co-founder, how much equity should you offer them? It's less important what the exact numbers are and more important that you have a plan, budget and rationale for the company's equity over time. This will be explored in greater detail in the "E" for Equity chapter.

D is for Demand

Identifying market demand is important for success as an entrepreneur. Many people have had great ideas without ever finding customers. While it's nice to imagine building a better mousetrap and having the world beat a path to your door, history has shown us many technologically superior products that never won their share of the market. It's been argued that BetaMax was the better video player, while VHS became the industry standard for many years. In 1985 Coca-Cola famously switched its formula to New Coke. The sweeter version for the drink was rejected in the marketplace and the company returned to its original recipe.

For a company to be successful it must connect its products and services to customers. This involves more than just providing quality. There must be an understanding of the marketplace, of consumer demographics, of the competitive landscape and a potential for growth. Apple reached the top because its company culture went beyond just shipping cool products. Apple's deep commitment to innovation, product design and a top-notch customer experience combined to make profits soar.

Creating demand is more than advertising and market research. Advertising alone does not create demand, but instead brings the attention of the greater population to your product or service. Creating demand is difficult and leaves many start-ups lost without reaching revenue goals. Customers are not always aware that they want a new product and thus the product marketing strategies must be intertwined with education and product development. Henry Ford famously said, "If I had asked people what they wanted, they would have said faster horses."

Commoditization is another problem that faces many companies. Too many products and services appear to provide similar solutions, supported by advertising and marketing. While showing always is better than telling, this is not easy to do in a world with limited access to customers' eyes and ears.

This is where creating demand through word-of-mouth marketing and creating legions of customers as "fans" will have a real impact. Simply having a Facebook page or a Twitter account does not serve up a fan base. Getting others to talk about your company means providing experiences that make people feel good about participating in your community.

Entrepreneurs should make it a priority to bust out of the impression of being a commodity. Invest in creating a USP or Unique Selling Proposition that matches target customer values to the unique features, benefits and services you offer. A USP is a claim the competition cannot make. There is always more demand for something unique.

Create an integrated marketing strategy that combines educating the consumer, cultivating visibility and delivering at the highest level. Marketing research can determine which products or services may be of interest to customers, but there is an element of risk that leads to the top levels of success. Research alone cannot guarantee people will buy what you have to sell. And even if they do line up to purchase your products, past actions of customers does not mean they will keep buying. This process should not stop once your company achieves success, as customer needs will change. Successful entrepreneurs pay attention and seek ways to get out in front of new trends.

Identifying who your customer is, providing them with value, keeping them engaged, and getting them to be advocates for your company leads to increased demand and profitability.

E is for Equity

Every entrepreneur wants to raise capital, but no one wants to give away equity. There are only 100 percentage points of equity to be had in a business, and by the time you give some to Uncle Fred who loaned you some money, a stranger for giving you a cool domain name and your lawyer for drawing up your incorporation papers, there isn't much left.

Proper planning for your equity helps. Create a plan for how much you're going to sell to investors (if any), give to employees, and use for other purposes. This is one instance where author Steven Covey's habit "begin with the end in mind" is useful. Figure out where you want to end up, and then make a plan for how to get there.

There are different ways to manage the equity. Entrepreneurs can build up multi-million dollar businesses over a longer period of time and retain more equity. They control the growth rates to levels that allow profits to be re-invested and don't accept outside capital investors. Entrepreneurs can also give away lots of equity to raise money and use the cash to grow their piece of the pie bigger and achieve liquidity faster.

To research companies' equity structures, find a company's Initial Public Offering (IPO) registration form named S/1 by the Securities and Exchange Commission (SEC). It will tell you how much equity the founders and early employees retained before going public. You'll find an incredible amount of variety, and there's probably an interesting back story to each one.

If you're starting a "lifestyle business," then you probably don't want anybody else to have any equity in your company at all. A lifestyle business is one where your goal is to provide a level of income or freedom sufficient to support your personal lifestyle instead of the lifestyles of many others as well. Realistically, most people will not even want equity in your business.

The only reason a non-owner is interested in equity is the possibility of a sale down the road, or a "liquidity event," which is a chance to turn their equity into money. For a lifestyle business, presumably there is no liquidity event.

There are some exceptions, of course. If your business ends up generating significant net profits, or essentially cash in excess of that required to re-invest in the business, you could declare a dividend. Dividends have preferential tax treatment (at least at the time of this writing), and are paid to shareholders on a price-per-share basis.

The most common pitfalls in equity distribution are undocumented and poorly defined promises of it. Imagine that you're just about to close on a round of investment capital for your business when the investors figure out that you promised Cousin Clyde 3% of the company in exchange for office space. The first problem is that it's not backed up by any signed documentation and the second problem is that you haven't defined the equity. Is 3% of the company in options, common stock, preferred stock, or warrants? Is that 3% of the company its value the day before it goes public, on the day you made the promise, or on any day of Cousin Clyde's choosing?

When it comes to spending money on professional services, don't go cheap. It's money well spent. Create your equity plan and find a trusted legal professional to help you execute on it. You will never regret doing so.

F is for Fail Fast

Rarely does something invoke such a varied level of emotions as does failure. In some cultures it's a source of shame and in others it's almost a badge of honor. Failing isn't fun, but when you're an entrepreneur you need to fail, and you need to fail quickly.

"Fail Fast" is the unofficial slogan of Austin, Texas-based Capital Factory, an accelerator program for early stage technology startup companies. It sounds rather odd, but failing is one key to success

Most managers will not offer instant praise when you walk in and say, "Hey boss, I failed at this." However, enlightened managers will instead focus on what you learned from the failure, challenge your assumptions on the root causes, and then ask you what you're going to change in order to make your next attempt a success. Henry Ford once said,

"Failure is simply an opportunity to begin again, this time more intelligently."

Don't Just Fail, Do it Quickly

While failing is not foundational to entrepreneurship, failing fast is. Failing means you're pushing the boundaries and learning. Let's say that you want to learn how to be a great checkers player. Your opponent is making moves at random and you win every time. Do you learn anything about checkers? No, because you didn't fail.

The "fast" part of this is just as important as the failure itself. If your online ads aren't converting to sales, you want to know as soon as possible so that you can stop wasting your money. The faster you figure out that something doesn't work, the faster you can learn from it and try something a little different.

In addition, if you spend a lot of time and effort on something and then it fails, you will have a harder time admitting defeat, taking your lumps and moving on. You will have too much of an emotional investment in the work to readily admit failure.

Failing can injure you, and failing slowly just adds insult to the injury.

Fail Quick, Fail Small

There is also a corollary to this maxim which is "fail small." In order to fail small, you have to iterate rapidly. If you spend $10 million to build a rocket and it explodes on the launch pad, you probably have no idea what the problem was. Was it a faulty ignition switch? Fuel instability? Who can tell? It's hard to learn anything by failing big, and it's expensive too!

As an entrepreneur, once you start this process of failing quickly and trying again, the less impact the word "fail" will have on you.

G is for Growth

Growth is one of the most exciting aspects of a new company. Growth is like dynamite; it can be used to build a bridge, or it can kill you. It's one of the things we work hard to achieve and it also creates numerous challenges to overcome if your company is to survive.

Finding enough quality people in the timeline you need them is one of the top challenges of rapid growth. With fast growth, you need good people pronto. You hire every qualified person you're familiar with from previous companies, but then you have to begin branching out. Hiring people that you don't personally know and cannot vouch for creates risk. This is where you have to rely on great processes, and the ability of your earlier hires to identify a good cultural fit.

Scaling processes is another major challenge. A startup sportswear company in the early 1990s rapidly grew because of its unique and popular clothing. Early in the company's history, they moved from being a niche clothing company to a mainstream clothing manufacturer. The owners negotiated a substantial deal with a major retailer to grow the company's revenues by over 30x with this one single deal! The company came up with new designs demanded by the retailer, and executives flew to China to negotiate the manufacture, assembly, shipping, and delivery of the orders. Every process in the supply chain was stretched, and every system maxed out. Unfortunately that also meant that the timeline also stretched out. This caused a delay in product delivery, which is not an option for clothing retailers who are slaves to seasons and styles. At the end of the day, the entire product ended up in the company's warehouse, unable to be sold, tying up all of the company's capital and borrowing capacity. Growth killed the company. The entrepreneurs went from paper millionaires to bankruptcy.

Growth and other internal company challenges are far more likely to kill your company than competition. If you haven't heard about the Startup Genome Project, it's worth looking up. Researchers on the project benchmarked 3,200 startup companies and concluded that one major reason why high-growth technology startups fail is premature scaling. Entrepreneurs spend time and money on scale issues far too early in the lifecycle of the business. Some eager, well-funded companies are charging quickly into the marketplace and hiring people without the matching business model maturity. Experienced entrepreneurs rely on the mantra "Hire slowly, fire quickly." In reality, it's much easier said than done.

At the beginning, when entrepreneurs think about all the threats to the survival of their company, they typically consider competition, speed to market, and other people copying their idea. But the benchmarking studies show that it's more likely to be lack of product/market fit, and premature scaling (which leads to capital depletion).

H is for Home Life

Being an entrepreneur has a direct impact on those closest to you. Working for a company brings many advantages and disadvantages, as you have a sense of job security but not necessarily the freedoms that come with being your own boss. Entrepreneurship has a different impact: work hours and security can be all over the map, while the freedoms you might expect are not always present in the early stages of starting your venture. The responsibilities and pressures of growing a business mean that your family has to be part of your work life or they may feel squeezed out during the times when you are focused on work issues.

Your personal life can easily become intermingled with your business when you are starting or running your own company. Regardless of whether you arc a "solo-preneur" or leading a larger corporation, it can be difficult to use the "off switch" when you get home. Being self-aware of how engaged you are at home is important, as with today's technologies it's easy to remain plugged into work.

In the growth phase of a business money can be tight, which means sacrifices at home. However, those who create successful and sustainable companies often have financial windfalls that can more than compensate for the lean times. But nobody enjoys sacrificing at the time, and thus a spouse and children must be included in conversations about the focus and purpose of the entrepreneur's efforts or it is easy for people to feel cheated by any lifestyle hit. The three, five or ten years it can take to realize the upside may feel like a lifetime for the family.

Additionally, if you make the leap from employee to entrepreneur after you have a family, it might not be the lifestyle that your spouse and children expect.

Be sure that everyone at home understands the realities of living with an entrepreneur. While the long hours for business can take a toll, the entrepreneur can create a flex schedule that allows them to drive carpool, coach sports teams and leave town for long weekends. If work becomes overwhelming, it's easy to let the home-life responsibilities slip, but making family time a priority is the only way to stay engaged in the day-to-day functions of a family.

Many entrepreneurs are driven by a dream, but if those around them don't share the dream it can create conflicting priorities between home and work. Communication and clear expectations between family members is paramount to making sure that there is not additional stress added to the home-front.

Including your family in the business is one way to make sure everyone has buy-in. This does not mean your husband or wife needs to be employed at the company, but everyone should know what is happening with growth of the organization. Even young children will better understand when mommy or daddy is gone on a business trip when they know what it is their parent does for a living.

There is a lot written about work / life balance, but there is never real balance. Knowing our purpose at work and at home can make the tough choices easier. While being honest with our co-workers, our family and ourselves will not solve all the problems, it can moderate the misunderstandings and expectations.

I is for Innovation

A company's ability to innovate is its only sustainable competitive advantage.

One of the most famous and prolific proponents of business strategy is the Harvard Business School's Michael Porter. In the 1980s he wrote that the basic types of competitive advantage were product differentiation and product cost.[1] Over the years, as his research progressed, he focused increasingly on innovation writing things like "Innovation is the central issue in economic prosperity." If you had to explain, in one word, the difference between incredibly successful Apple and other companies in strategy decay, such as Research In Motion (RIM) and Nokia, it would be innovation.

Discussions of innovation go hand-in-hand with competitive advantage. Entrepreneur Jason Cohen, founder and CEO of WP Engine, defines

---

[1] *Competitive Advantage,* The Free Press, 1985

competitive advantage as "something that cannot be built or bought." Startup companies frequently cite things like industry knowledge, clever pieces of code, or business relationships as their competitive advantage. Put up against Jason's definition, this could be seen as misguided.

Peter Drucker, legendary author of more than 20 books on management, once said, "Innovation is the specific instrument of entrepreneurship, the act that endows resources with a new capacity to create wealth."[2]

In your new business venture there is an interesting middle ground between less innovative but understandable, and highly innovative but risky. Let's look at both extremes to help understand where the middle exists, and what will appeal to potential investors in your business.

On one end of the spectrum, imagine you are pitching investors on your business and the model is similar to other companies. Your investors

---

[2] *Innovation and Entrepreneurship*,HarperBusiness, 1985. p 30

understand the industry, the cash flow model is predictable, and you've thought of a new twist that hasn't broadly been adopted by the industry yet. Your deal should be a bit hit with investors, right? This is a generally safe bet. The word safe translates to low returns.

On the other end of the spectrum, let's suppose that your new venture is taking a dramatically different and largely unproven approach to solving a really big problem in a really big market. Your product has worked on a limited basis, but still needs significant R&D for it to work in all instances. If it works, the entire industry will be using your products, and the company will be worth billions.

While these examples may be at two extremes, it's important to understand the dilemma that investors generally face. If you want exceptional returns, you have to take exceptional risks. Sometimes these exceptional risks really do pay off.

When Google started to look for venture funding, they had a difficult time finding it. The market already had several dominant search engines: Yahoo, Excite and Alta Vista. What investor in their right mind wants to invest in the 10th search engine in the market? Google's approach was radically different, unproven and had never been done before. Today they are the market leader in search.

If you're looking for a high return, you probably want your new business to be on the higher end of the innovative spectrum yet not so high as to appear incredibly risky. Think big and have a reasonable path of small victories you can build on to get you to the big vision.

With any luck, you can apply innovation to your business in a tempered, yet progressive manner. Apple Computer is frequently cited as a model of innovative products. Founder Steve Jobs is quoted as saying "It's not the customer's job to know what they want." It seems that the true innovators in American history, people like Henry Ford, had a gift for staying one step ahead of their customers.

J is for Jobs

There are many reasons for starting your own company. Growing your business usually requires hiring people to scale with the growth. As you onboard employees, you are putting people to work. Politicians should be praising entrepreneurs because the economic activity of hiring people is the coveted act of job creation that every elected official pledges to drive. It's the combined hiring acts of thousands of entrepreneurs around the country that drive down the unemployment rates. According to the US Small Business Administration, small businesses generated 65% of net new jobs from 1993 to 2009.[3] Half of the people in the private sector in the United States work for small businesses.

Hiring also has some consequences. Most people start off with just themselves, and the working alone and from home stage may last a long time.

[3] U.S. Dept. of Labor, Bureau of Labor Statistics, Business Employment Dynamics; Advocacy-funded research by Zoltan Acs, William Parsons and Spencer Tracy, 2008.

Eventually the time comes to hire, and the difference is dramatic. Suddenly your business has 100% more hours to get things done. You've also doubled the number of good ideas your team can come up with, and the number of solutions to problems.

Watching your employees grow professionally can also be a source of pride. The experience of being on the ground floor of a growing company can sometimes create an entrepreneurial spark in people! There is nothing more rewarding than seeing someone grow professionally, giving them more and more responsibility, helping them succeed, and watching them eventually break off and start their own company.

K is for Knowledge

The old saying that "knowledge is power" is not just a cliché. What you know will have a tangible impact on the long-term growth of your company. Knowledge in three areas is key: your industry, your products/services (and how they impact the customers) and your own experience level.

Being well versed in your industry is important to deciding where to focus your growth efforts. Competitive analysis and a grasp of historical cycles allow the entrepreneur to make the tough choices with regard to Research & Development, expansion and marketing investments. Industry knowledge also helps in attracting key hires from the competition.

Understanding your products and services helps you stay relevant. Things change fast. What sold yesterday may not sell tomorrow.

It's important to offer what your clients want and deem necessary. Offerings can become obsolete quickly, and the tools that customers use to gather information can undermine buyers' loyalty.

Recognizing your level of experience will serve you well. The thrill of being your own boss does not replace the need to be able to effectively manage employees, understand sales and marketing, or deal with unhappy customers. When you are clear about the areas you need to improve you can either focus on learning the missing skills or hire people who can compensate.

Know what you know, and what you don't know. Entrepreneurial knowledge will help you avoid common missteps, and make decisions which positively impact your future.

L is for Lean

We could speak to lean in terms of bootstrapping, capital efficiency or building your business out of your garage. In this case, however, we're going to talk about iterating your business model very rapidly.

The 1990s Business School mentality would promote a process that goes something like this: write up a lengthy business plan, do some research, develop a product, then market and sell it. With this approach you won't know if the model will work until you've already invested a lot of time and money.

The Lean Approach, popularized for startups by Silicon Valley start-up pioneer Eric Ries, originated in manufacturing. Ries suggests that wc find pcople who have a problem worth solving, get them to commit to paying if you can solve their problem, then go develop the offering. Done right, your product or service will be on target because it was conceived with the customer at the heart of the process.

So, how can you get someone to pay you in advance for solving a problem? The answer is that if they're not willing to pay in advance, then there must not be enough pain involved to make it worth solving. Go find another problem to solve.

Getting close to the problem and real-life customers requires you to get out of the office! Entrepreneur Sam Decker, founder of Mass Relevance, an Austin, Texas based social experience platform, uses the phrase "breathing customer oxygen." Put yourself in their shoes to give you some perspective on what their problems are. You'll create much more value spending time with your customers than you will sitting behind your desk.

Another foundational belief of Lean companies is that of measurement and metrics, especially when it comes to the assumptions you are making about your product or service. Assumptions are guesses you make in the absence of real information. When you are designing your product, you're making hundreds of assumptions about how people will use it, what features they will find useful, and the value it will provide them. Assumptions just sit there until you either validate or invalidate them.

Using a Lean Approach will help to keep you from building products that nobody wants or needs, let alone will pay for.

M is for Money

Taking the risk of being an entrepreneur is for the reward, which for most is money, isn't it? Yes and no?

Starting a business solely for financial gain could lead to much frustration. Is it really money that you're after or is it the things money provides like the means to travel, set up a foundation to benefit your favorite cause, or put your kids through college debt-free? Everyone has their own motivations for wanting to be an entrepreneur.

For high-profile entrepreneurs such as Mark Cuban, Richard Branson or Larry Ellison, money is a convenient and easy way to keep score. *Forbes* and *Fortune* love to print lists that make it easy to compare who is worth more, or has the highest salary. Scientists have discovered that when someone makes more money than a colleague, the "reward centers" in their brain fire. It's no wonder, then, that money makes a convenient measuring stick for self-esteem.

Do you have what it takes to be financially successful? Do you have enough knowledge to grow a thriving business? Are you smart enough to make a lot of money?

These questions are asked a lot, but, believe it or not, there is no relationship between IQ and wealth. IQ measures what someone could achieve with their intelligence. It doesn't mean they will achieve anything in particular, or that what they achieve will result in financial gain.

In a startup, making a dollar and saving a dollar achieve the same result. Let's look at some ways that a startup can save money easily.

> *Support Programs.* When speaking with your service providers (bankers, PR firms, and attorneys) ask if they have any special programs or discounts for startups. You would be surprised how many do.

Just Ask. You never know until you ask. Does this printer ever go on sale? Is there a coupon for this item? Have you ever seen a lower interest rate for a loan like this? Is there a way to get the same thing accomplished for less money? You might be surprised by the answer.

Pay Cash for a Discount. For people who are used to being paid on terms, offer them cash today for a discount. Even with 30- or 60-day terms you're going to make a bunch of money on interest at today's rates. Doctors that have to file insurance paperwork and wait months to get paid sometimes offer discounts for cash payments at the time of service.

Ask for Terms. The financial engineering at Dell has been written about extensively in business textbooks. The company demands 80-day terms from its component suppliers, yet gets paid up front for the computers it sells. Dell has found a creative way to finance its business on the backs of its suppliers. If your client isn't going to pay you within 30 days for a project, ask the person that is doing the artwork for that project to also give you 30-day terms and you won't be out-of-pocket in the interim.

Trade-out. It happens all the time in local businesses. A restaurant buys \$500 in advertising spend, paying \$250 in cash and a \$250 credit at the restaurant. It's a great deal for the restaurant, as their cost basis for a \$250 dinner is far less than \$250. They get a \$500 ad for \$400. It's not a terrible deal for the local paper either. Instead of a \$250 bonus, they could give an employee the \$250 restaurant gift card. This technique is fairly common in the service industry.

While money is important, it may not be the sole purpose for becoming an entrepreneur. While intelligence does not guarantee that your business will thrive, finding ways to conserve capital is also a smart path to success.

N is for Networking

Growing a business can be an all-encompassing experience. Many entrepreneurs put so much attention into their venture that they forget to make, grow and keep their business relationships. The immediacy of issues surrounding funding, clients, employees, vendors, regulations, and product specifications leaves little space for things that do not scream measurable ROI.

Much of the advice around productivity involves identifying the purpose of every activity on the calendar. With limited hours in the day, and the intensity necessary to run a company, it becomes easy for an entrepreneur to push the cultivation of relationships to "nice to have activity" from a "must have activity". While time is precious, it is important for the entrepreneur to remember that all opportunities come from people. If you have the right network in place, most of your challenges can be solved through a strategic phone call or two.

However, you cannot wait until you have a need to build a relationship. If the only time you show up at business events or place those calls is when you're in crisis, it'll be difficult to get a response. Building a network takes time and, even in our fast -paced digital world, you cannot create a friendship simply by sending a LinkedIn request.

The introductions made by those with whom you have established long-term and mutually beneficial relationships can lead you to the right investor, lawyer, banker, accountant, or other vendor. It's through people that you can quickly find the employee you need to hire to take your business to the next level. There are no short cuts to meaningful connections with people who know, like and trust you, and that understand your business.

Entrepreneurs sometimes make the mistake of only wanting to network with other entrepreneurs. CEOs often seek out groups that only admit other CEOs and that can be very limiting for several reasons. First, another business owner will not tell you that they have the best receptionist or sales manager for fear they may get lured away to other companies. Second, you cannot grow and learn when everyone is just like you. There must be diversity in your network that includes race, religion, gender and age. Include diversity of job titles and industries if you want access to a variety of information.

Out of sight is out of mind. Even when you are busy launching the business or a new product, you cannot disappear from your community. There will come a time when you will need other people, and you cannot expect people to be sitting around waiting for you to call. You must always cultivate the connection.

O is for Overtime

There is no over-time when you run the business; there is only all-the-time.

The number of hours that entrepreneurs put into launching and growing their ventures can be daunting. When you are responsible for every little detail, the number of issues that you will need to address can be overwhelming. Product and service issues, accounting, legal, HR, sales, marketing, facilities, customer service, IT, vendor relations, and more ultimately land on your desk needing attention.

Ignoring any problem and wishing it will go away will only cause it to fester into a bigger concern. Delegating can also be a problem in the early stages, as until you have experienced leaders on your team, there might not be anyone to take on the responsibility for making decisions. Entrepreneurs must be decisive and action-oriented or they will get caught in the loop of ever-shrinking amounts of time and a never-ending to-do list.

People who are committed to building their dream are rarely burdened by the amount of work it takes. When creating a sustainable entity is fused into your core, the hours do not seem like work. People who easily tire of the tedious parts of the business may be flirting with failure. The intimate pieces of being entrepreneurial must be in your soul to keep pushing you forward when times get tough.

It is common for entrepreneurs to get frustrated with the monotonous parts of running the company. The reality is, when you are emotionally engaged in anything, it can cause volatility at times. There are many examples of great leaders who have outrageous tempers and outbursts. Being head down in one cause will make it hard to see the rest of your world with a realistic perspective. Keeping a balance is something you must do with intention.

Be prepared for days when you question why no one else can solve a problem or lighten your load.

Know that growing a business can be very lonely, even when you have close friends, a supportive family and dedicated employees. Strive to make early hires that are also entrepreneurial, willing and excited to roll up their sleeves and work long hours. Clock-watchers will dumbfound an entrepreneur.

Surround yourself with peers who are also entrepreneurs. There are many formal organizations that exist to create networking and education opportunities for business owners. Being around others who are tackling similar issues is a fast way to understand the shared strains of leadership. Entrepreneurs Organization (EO), Vistage and Young Presidents Organization (YPO) are just a few examples. Your local Chamber of Commerce or trade association will also know of other groups where you can participate.

The old adage, "All work and no play makes Jack a dull boy" is true for entrepreneurs. The excitement of the business can cause people to ignore everything else. While there are no real days off when you are running a company, you can be proactive in carving out time for the people you love and the outside activities that re-charge your batteries. One technique for accomplishing this would be to put personal commitments on your calendar just like a business appointment. The rapid pace of doing work that you enjoy can make it easy to lose track of time. Invest time to cultivate your relationships, including the relationship with yourself.

Nobody said being an entrepreneur was easy. There is neither overtime pay nor sick days. However, if you really love what you are doing, you will not care.

P is for Pivot

In dance, a pivot is defined as a 180-degree turn. Hopefully your business never turns 180 degrees because that would send it back in the direction it came from. But every business makes some sort of pivot, or course correction, on its path to success. Ideally you don't have to change direction drastically, but minor course corrections are actually a good thing. Why is that?

In theory, you're listening to customer feedback as part of growing your business. During this time you're making a series of course corrections that lead you to product/market fit and a successful revenue model. Ending up in a slightly different place doesn't mean you've failed at your stated goal. Instead, it's like going on vacation and, instead of visiting all the museums that you intended, you end up having a wonderful dinner with some local people that you just met. You couldn't have planned for this at the start, but you still had an enjoyable evening. If nothing else, entrepreneurs learn to be flexible.

Many businesses started out in one industry and ended up in a different one.

- Consider Nokia. The company, then named Finnish Rubber Works, started in 1898 by manufacturing in the mills on the river. The rivers were used for hydroelectric power, and power was transmitted with wire and cable. It took many years, but the company that began making rubber ended up in the electronics business.

- One of the largest global IT outsourcers is the Indian company Wipro. Wipro is the abbreviation for Western India Palm Refined Oil.

- Southern Pacific Railroad saw a sharp decline in revenue as overland trucking became faster and more flexible than shipping by rail. More than a hundred years ago the railroads acquired the thin little strip of land beneath and adjacent to their tracks. Southern Pacific built a telecommunications subsidiary and started burying optical fiber next to their tracks. With the rise of telephone and internet traffic, the fiber became more profitable than the trains and Southern Pacific's telecom subsidiary turned into a little company named Qwest Communications.

- After serving in WWII, a young Italian mechanic started building tractors out of leftover equipment from the war. By the mid 1950s he had built one of the largest agricultural equipment manufacturers in the country. The wealth from his success in the tractor business fueled Ferruccio Lamborghini's interest in cars, and the rest is history.

- There are some modern day examples of pivots in the technology industry. Some guys in Silicon Valley started with a podcast directory website. In their spare time they wrote a short messaging service product which today is known as Twitter.

- Pixar spent many years making software that produced 3D animations, and their short films were just demos of the software's capabilities. Today Pixar is a movie studio and a division of The Disney Companies.

It's rare that companies, especially tech companies, come out of a three- to five-year growth period in the exact same business they started in. The art of the pivot goes hand-in-hand with the chapter L on Lean, iterating your entire business model for success. Remain flexible and keep your eye out for a profitable pivot, no matter what business you're in right now.

Q is for Quitting

We've all seen the entrepreneurs on the cover of Fortune, or pictures of young internet billionaires aboard their yachts on social media. They hit the lottery. They had the right thing, in the right place, at the right time. Yes, they worked hard as well, and chance favors the prepared entrepreneur, but they are the minority. I've never met an entrepreneur who didn't think about giving it up at least once, and sometimes multiple times a day. But who wants to be a quitter?

The spirit of an entrepreneur drives you to succeed even through failures. However, there are times when, if you can't make changes quickly or in such a way to sustain, walking away can make sense. One example is a local pizza parlor owner and operator with a franchise location. Everything seemed great. He was making more than $100,000/ year so he had a comfortable life. He was his own boss and made all the decisions for the business.

What could be better? In reality, a lot. The business owned him. He worked six long days a week. He received all the shipments for fear an employee might walk off with cases of beer. If someone called in sick, he waited tables or cooked. He was the first person to open the doors and the last person to close them. The business wasn't so profitable that he could hire a full-time general manager, so he was the owner, operator and the whatever-else-needed-to-be-done person. If sales that month were light because of the economy, a competitor running a special across the street, or a cold snap kept people from dining out, he wrote a personal check to make payroll. And what about time off? Any departure of more than a couple days was virtually impossible.

Even in a high-growth technology business, the story is the same. Investors are constantly sending you news clippings of your competitors' accomplishments or doom and gloom economy editorials. If you're not breaking bread with a customer, potential customer, investor or potential investor, it's likely you're chowing down on fast food at your desk or in your car on the way to a meeting. You leverage personal friendships to encourage people to come work for your risky new company, and those employees want to send their kids to private school. Yet you're never sure if the sales numbers this quarter are going to meet the goal.

Your mother is bragging to all of her friends that your company is going to be the next big IPO. Your rock star salesperson just quit. And your largest competitor just acquired another company and is investing millions to make it successful. At the same time your co-founder is saying she's burnt out and isn't working evenings and weekends like she used to. All of these things can happen, sometimes frequently or all at once.

It's easy to quit when people are constantly telling you it won't work, it can't work, you don't have the right team, they don't have confidence in you, there's no market for your product, and the competition is too big. They say it's always darkest right before the dawn, but you need to know when to quit, on your terms, for the right reasons.

R is for Resilience

An entrepreneur will be tested. Along the way they will be pushed and prodded. They will fall down. There will be days when they will question their resolve. At times they will wonder if all the sacrifices are worth the long hours and constant pressure. It's not a matter of if an entrepreneur will face tough times, but when.

This is where resilience comes into play. Successful entrepreneurs must have the ability to return to their original excitement and dedication of growing their business after facing down adversity.

Resiliency does not happen by accident. An individual makes the choice to bounce back no matter how they are bent and stretched. Being in charge, dealing with employee issues, measuring client satisfaction, winning investors, managing burn rates, adhering to government regulations, and countless other responsibilities can push anyone to the breaking point.

Stress can be a strong opponent, especially for a first-time entrepreneur. To combat this, the entrepreneur must counter with a long-term vision, a strong belief in self, emotional control and external social support.

Long-term vision: Knowing that your commitment to the venture is bigger than any short-term setback will help you look past a current situation. Being aware of the goal will make it easier to navigate yourself toward a solution to the problem. There are always options when you are clear on the destination.

Belief in self: Doubt can quickly undermine anyone. Successful entrepreneurs are sure that they will find success. This confidence gets them out of bed on those mornings that they want to pull the covers over their head.

Control of emotions: When we deal with other people, there are often emotions involved. When we allow negative feelings to take over, we can make poor choices. Hurt feelings, jealousy, embarrassment, disappointment, anger, fear, guilt and other emotional responses can cloud judgment and lead to poor decisions.

External social support: When facing difficulties we can discover resolve in the experiences of others. Having a network of other business professionals whom you can turn to will always be a great resource for an entrepreneur. A formal or informal group of advisors can guide you through the muddy waters.

Resilience is important. You will get knocked around and down, but you must be being able to get up and be stronger than before. Rising up and moving forward is the only option for the successful entrepreneur.

S is for Sales

If you run the business, you must always be selling. This means selling the offering, selling the brand, selling the power of your team and selling yourself. Your organization's future relies on sales; without revenue there will be no business. Even if you receive initial funding to launch, without sustainable income, the business can't survive.

There are no shortcuts or magic marketing strategies that will cause the phone to ring. Having a clear approach toward the value of a sales process will be a constant reminder that new and repeat clients matter.

For entrepreneurs who do not have a sales or marketing background, the process of client acquisition can seem like the dark side of running the business. Websites, advertising, mobile apps, social media, and hoping for a miracle are not solid revenue generation strategies. If the entrepreneur is not confident in their ability to sell, they will need to make a strategic hire early on. The sales leader and entrepreneur will be working very closely together, so it must be someone with whom they can establish and maintain a good personal relationship. This individual's characteristics will vary depending on the industry, but if the goal is to achieve short-term sales, experience and industry contacts are a must.

Entrepreneurs with a sales background are often way out front in discovering prospects and driving revenue, but they cannot do it alone. Selling is a full-time job and the entrepreneur has too many other responsibilities that can be at odds with the demands of cultivating clients. The primary function of the salesperson is to educate prospective clients and convert them into paying customers.

Companies that lead with sales will often see faster growth than those who push their revenue generation priorities to the sidelines. Tracking the entire process, from lead generation, to movement through the pipeline, to the final sale, must be constantly monitored by the entrepreneur. It's very easy to pin the hopes of a company on a few prospects, but if they do not pan out, there must be an understanding of what else is in play.

The days of "if you build a better mousetrap, the world will beat a path to your door" are long gone. Having great products means nothing if you can't move them. Great sales professionals are paid well, as their success at delivering new business is paramount to the sustainability and growth of a company. To succeed in a sales role takes tenacity, the ability to handle rejection, an understanding of human nature, strong communications skills, and empathy. Not every possible customer will buy in a timely fashion, or even at all.

Not everyone is cut out for sales. Surround yourself with good advisors and a solid team, including a knowledgeable sales leader and you increase your chances at sustainable success.

T is for Team

Most successful businesses begin with an initial great idea. However, without the right people to execute that idea, it will go nowhere profitable.

Consider this:

- An "A" team with an "A" idea will always get funded.
- An "A" team with a "B" idea will usually get funded.
- A "B" team with an "A" idea will rarely get funded
- A "B" team with a "B" idea will never get funded.

Why Teams are so Important

There are several reasons why the team is important.

First, a company with just one person is risky. What if that person gets a one-in-a-million job offer? They will leave their startup dreams behind, and investors holding the bag. Worse yet, what if that person gets hit by a bus? There is no more business.

Second, no one has a monopoly on good ideas. As great as you think your ideas are, there is no way for one person to dream up all the good ideas in the universe. For that you need help. In addition, ideas often build upon each other, as we discussed with Brainstorming.

Third, just like a three-legged stool, you are seeking stability. Support in numbers with a balance of ideas and strengths mixed together creates a solid foundation. When thinking of team, consider the following African proverb, "If you want to go fast, go alone, but if you want to go far, go together."

Filling Out the Company

Beyond the founders, the first 20 people that you bring onto your team are going to set the tone and establish the behaviors for the whole organization. Your company's culture will have a direct impact in how you attract future hires and interact with customers. Hiring the right people early on is critical to your company's success. One thing you have going for you in the early days is that you can hire people you know, have worked with before and can personally attest to their ability to perform. Between you and your co-founders, you should be able to make a short list of people who get things done, are likable, and have a passion for their work. Try to hire from that pool first, and then tap into referrals.

Referrals can help grow the company but it's up to you to do the in-depth interviews, background checks, fit, and skills assessments. You are no longer hiring people that you have worked with personally before so your hiring process has to become more exploratory as you seek the right mix of experience and personality. Naturally you're going to make some hiring mistakes, but learning to identify good candidates will become easier with time. If you are growing fast you'll be in a position where you need to hire a larger group of quality people quickly. Regardless of speed, ensure you're making decisions for the long-term because hiring mistakes at the earliest stage are the most costly.

U is for Up Front

If you want to start a business, you need to prepare up front. While there are a lot of aspects to running a company that require you to be nimble, the more you prepare before you begin, the better you'll be able to handle the inevitable surprises. The journey of entrepreneurship requires both a mix of pre-planning as well as flexibility.

Having a vision is important. While most entrepreneurs will admit that their initial business plan was not an accurate map, few investors or advisors are keen to commit without a plan. The business plan is still an important tool to launching in most industries.

There is no way, unless you are a clairvoyant, to predict the changes in your company, industry or the economy. Too many variables exist in the real world. Engineering is an exact science that requires perfection or buildings and bridges could collapse.

Entrepreneurship is the opposite, often needing some heroic bending of rules and other flexibility to achieve success.

Someone who started a business in 2008 may not have foreseen the severe recession that came shortly thereafter. Their plan would quickly have become obsolete, but having a clear vision for the company could allow them to better navigate the tough decisions. When you think about your plan up front, be sure to imagine multiple scenarios, even though you can never predict every possibility.

Growing a business often takes more time and more money than anticipated, even with the most realistic planning. Be prepared to extend, maybe double, your original estimates. If your upfront projections call for three years and $500,000 to profitability, consider what you will need if the reality is six years and $1 million. Your plan may assume that three salespeople will achieve your sales goal, but the reality may be that it takes five.

Acknowledge going in that you can easily get buried with the small things and commit early in the process to putting your energy into activities that allow you to grow your business.

How you begin will have a major impact on how you finish. Invest the time to plan and prepare for an ample timeline and financial resources. While no amount of up-front planning will eliminate the obstacles, you will be less surprised by the hardships when they occur.

V is for Vision

Even though V is toward the end of the alphabet, vision is one of the most important things for entrepreneurs to have; it's right up there with Innovation. It's the one thing that separates the Steve Jobs and Richard Branson's of the world from everybody else. We're not talking about a crazy, far-out vision of people living on Mars here, just what's next or could be next.

Think about how the trends in technology and society will impact your area of expertise in the next three to five years. What has nobody else thought about yet? Wayne Gretzky is often quoted as saying, "A good hockey player plays where the puck is. A great hockey player plays where the puck is going to be."

Thinking Too Small

It's easy to get caught up thinking small as you do your first start-up. However, it helps to have a much bigger vision of where your company is headed.

Big thinking is what enabled Steve Jobs to lure John Sculley away from a bright and secure future at Pepsi. In Sculley's book Odyssey: Pepsi to Apple he said that Jobs asked him one pointed question, "Do you want to sell sugared water for rest of your life or do you want to come with me and change the world?"[4] This challenged Sculley to re-evaluate his career and join Apple, if only for a blip in time in Apple's history.

Thinking Too Big

Not every company has to change the world. It just has to be visionary for your industry.

[4] Harper & Rowe, New York. First edition. Copyright 1987. Page 90

Let's consider an ice cream shop. You've been in many typical chain ice cream stores where local teens work as cheap labor serving up scoop after scoop. And then there's Amy's Ice Cream Parlor in Austin. The ice cream is incredible tasting, made with quality, seasonal ingredients and the presentation is beautiful. The people who work there clearly enjoy dishing up your ice cream, wearing funny hats, beating candy bits into your ice cream, and flipping it behind their backs and into your cup. Amy founded the business and her vision has taken her far beyond the average chain ice cream storefront.

W is for Wisdom

Few people will admit to lacking wisdom. Most are self-confident in their ability to make decisions, regardless of reality. Wisdom is necessary to make consistent and appropriate judgments, yet it is not an attribute that is easy to gain or to self-determine. Lacking in wisdom is not how anyone wants to be viewed by their peers.

Age is often associated with wisdom, but for an entrepreneur, it has more to do with having an open mind and a realization that they do not instinctively hold all the answers. It's the decision-making process and the types of actions that are undertaken. Wisdom is gained by what you do between those birthdays.

Serial entrepreneurs surround themselves with people smarter than themselves because they know that wisdom can only come with meaningful experience. An entrepreneur discovers wisdom from being in the game. One Hit Wonders in business often have trouble recreating the same level of success. The skills that work for one entrepreneur are not the same as those that lead another to success. There are also changes that the entrepreneur must make from one business to the next.

Mistakes are part of the journey. Those who are considered wise have learned not only from the mistakes of others, but also from their own stumbles. Entrepreneurs are willing to take risks, and when their results come up short, they assess their methods and look for a way that will propel them toward a better outcome the next time.

Finding wisdom is deeply personal. Question everything and listen to others. You will know you are wise when other people say so, not when you think it's true.

X is for eXit

When you start your own company, the eventual goal is an exit. Entrepreneurs often dream of liquidity, obtaining the big money and never having to work again. There are two ways this happens; the most common is an acquisition and the least common is a public offering of your stock. Let's save the IPO for another book, and talk about an exit strategy ending in a sale.

Companies are Bought, not Sold

One common misperception is that at some point in the business lifecycle, an entrepreneur just puts their company on the auction block and sells it for a nice juicy price. Unfortunately, that can't be further from the truth. Open marketplaces for selling companies just don't exist. Even worse, there are business brokers who prey on the hopes and dreams of entrepreneurs.

If you set out to sell your company then you're immediately at a disadvantage. Instead, position your company so that your products or services are disruptive and superior to larger competitors. This makes you desirable and a leader with ongoing potential, which is what investors look for.

So, how do you position your company for purchase and how would you value it? There are three basic ways to value any company: cash flow, growth potential, and strategic value.

Cash Flow: Let's start with the least desirable, which is valuing your company based on cash flow. Assume that your company makes $10M per year in sales and puts $1M to the bottom line in earnings after taxes and depreciation. Standard discounted cash flow methods will value your business based on the cash flow, and the further out that potential cash is in future years, the bigger the discount on their value. In general, you can sell a company with flat growth for 6–7x your annual bottom line number, which in this case would be \$6M–\$7M.

Growth Potential: Taking that same \$10M per year in sales for this example your prior year's revenues were \$2M and \$4M. Your company is doubling sales (or slightly more) each year. You are now a growth company. Who even cares if you're making money? You can trim costs down the road when you're a \$50M company. How much money is this growth company worth? It's more like 2x–3x gross revenues, or \$20M–\$30M. This is far better than our previous example.

Strategic Value: Let's add a strategic multiplier to that second example. Envision a much larger company taking your product, giving it to their existing sales organization of 2,200 people internationally, and generating \$150M in additional sales revenue from it with little additional sales effort from those people. Your product is similar to existing products carried by the

> sales organization so they already know how to sell it, and are already talking to potential customers. With a strategic multiplier in effect, how much is your company worth now? The sky is the limit.

Which would you rather have, the $7M deal, the $30M deal, or the $100M deal?

The best advice here is to be a strategic acquisition to somebody, and to sell the company on a strong track record of revenue growth before the rate of growth year-over-year begins to decline. If you do it right, suitors will be calling on you long before you decide to sell.

Y is for Yes

The word "yes" frequently comes out of the mouths of entrepreneurs. These could mean taking a leap of faith to pursue a dream full-time, or starting a side business that allows testing abilities and ideas. People who are really called to being an entrepreneur will never be satisfied until they go for it.

It can be frightening. There are many unknowns. The pressure to succeed can be overwhelming. Family and friends may be discouraging. All these things make it difficult to go for it, and commit to yes.

If you have a yearning to be an entrepreneur, working for others will quietly get under your skin. Bosses and co-workers will disappoint you. You will second guess the decisions of others. Watching people start and grow companies will make you green with envy.

One way to get comfortable with becoming an entrepreneur is to surround yourself with other business owners. Get to know them professionally and socially while observing how they go about running their companies.

Those with a real entrepreneurial spirit are drawn together. In high-growth cities, there seems to be a willingness to exchange ideas, no matter if people are creating large companies or if they are solo-preneurs.

Contemplating your leap to entrepreneurship will allow you to be prepared when the right opportunity crosses your path. If you know what you want, then be ready to say yes.

Z is the End. There is no end to entrepreneurship.

Z may be the last letter of our alphabet, but if you have the drive to be an entrepreneur, there is no end point. Tenacity is a way of life, especially when facing tough obstacles along the way. While every idea does not necessarily succeed, entrepreneurs do not know the meaning of the words can't, won't or die.

There are many things that can happen to you and your company. Some are good, others are not as pleasant. Change is the only constant and adapting to that change is one of the most important skills in the world of entrepreneurial success.

Your company may fail. It could run out of money or you could decide to walk away. You may have an exit event. You may keep ownership of the company and turn the reins over to another person to take the business to the next level of growth.

No matter what the reason, people separated from their company often move quickly onto a new project. The journey is never over for those who are called to create. A real entrepreneur will simply find his or her next thing.

The new adventure could be another start-up, working for an established company, joining the world of non-profits, serving on boards, pursuing philanthropic interests or any of many other options. Regardless of what you do next, there is rarely retirement for those who follow the entrepreneurial path.

Conclusion

We hope you have enjoyed reading *The ABCs of Entrepreneurs*. While no book can comprehensively cover all of the topics that people encounter in starting and growing a company, it was our goal here to inspire you to think about the entrepreneurial road, and to expose you to some of the decisions you will have to make.

If you are already an entrepreneur, or seeking to launch out with your own venture, we encourage you to never stop learning. Join business organizations, network, read articles, and have engaging, in-depth conversations with other business owners.

Never forget that to make your entrepreneurial journey successful you will have to take actions. Experiment. Be honest with yourself. Gather data. Challenge assumptions. Push yourself and your team. You will make mistakes. Try not to repeat them and instead strive to make new and exciting mistakes! If you fail, regroup and look for other ways to carve out the path toward success.

Finally, remember to have fun!

Bryan Menell and Thom Singer
Austin, Texas

September 2013

About the Authors

A 2000 finalist for Ernst & Young's Entrepreneur of the Year award, **Bryan Menell** has 20 years of experience founding and growing Exact Systems (1991), Perficient (NASDAQ: PRFT) (1997), and Fusion Learning Systems (2001). Most recently he was the CEO of SubtleData.

He is active in Austin's technology scene, and is a co-founder and Mentor of Capital Factory, a seed stage mentoring program for technology companies. Bryan is the publisher of AustinStartup, which highlights emerging technology companies in Austin, and is an investor and advisor to a select group of companies. He also serves on the board of the Austin chapter of Texchange.

Bryan began his career in the San Francisco office of Andersen Consulting (now Accenture). He earned a bachelor's degree in Business / MIS at California State University at Chico.

Thom Singer is a professional speaker, sales trainer and the author of ten books on the power of business relationships, networking, presentation skills, and entrepreneurship. He has spent more than 20 years in sales, marketing, and business development roles with major corporations and law firms. He regularly consults with corporations, law firms and individuals on how to cultivate their personal brands and establish professional connections that will lead to more referral business.

His speaking includes impactful keynotes, break-outs sessions, training programs and the Conference Catalyst program. In this role he sets the tone for a meeting to be a place where people embrace the opportunity to create real and meaningful connections.

He and his wife, Sara, make their home in Austin, Texas, and are the parents of two highly spirited daughters.

Order Form

Fax orders: Fax this form to 800-558-2906
Telephone orders: Call 877-697-7323 (NYP-READ)
Please have your credit card ready.
Email orders: orders@newyearpublishing.com
Postal orders by credit card or personal check:

New Year Publishing, LLC
144 Diablo Ranch Court
Danville, CA 94506 USA

Name: ______________________________

Address: ______________________________

City/State/Zip: ______________________________

Telephone: ______________________________

Email: ______________________________

Quantity: ____ **@ $12.95 ABCs of Speaking**
Quantity: ____ **@ $12.95 ABCs of Networking**
Quantity: ____ **@ $12.95 ABCs of Networking (Spanish version)**
Quantity: ____ **@ $12.95 ABCs of Conferences**
Bulk discounts are available. Call New Year Publishing for additional information.
Sales tax: 9.25% for books shipped to California
Shipping: $5.95 per book
Total including applicable tax and shipping ______________
____Check ____Credit card

Card number: ______________________________

Name on card: ______________________________

Exp. date: ______________________________

Notes